SCOTT FRANCIS

FINANCIAL LITERACY HANDBOOK

Money Skills
for High School and Beyond

To my parents, Paul and Wendy, who amongst an infinite number of acts of generosity encouraged and supported both my education, and the development of my interest in the way money works. It is exciting to write a book that includes both of these interests of mine.

Published in 2023 by Amba Press, Melbourne, Australia
www.ambapress.com.au

© Scott Francis 2023

All rights reserved. No part of this book may be reproduced or transmitted in any form or by any means, electronic or mechanical, including photocopying, recording or by any information storage and retrieval system, without prior permission in writing from the publisher.

Cover design: Tess McCabe
Editor: Rica Dearman

ISBN: 9781922607188 (pbk)
ISBN: 9781922607195 (ebk)

A catalogue record for this book is available from the National Library of Australia.

Disclaimer: The material in this publication is in the nature of general comment only, and neither purports nor intends to be advice. Readers should not act on the basis of any matter in this publication without considering (and, if appropriate, taking) professional advice with due regard to their own particular circumstances. The author and publisher disclaim all and any liability to any person, whether a purchaser of this publication or not, in respect to anything and the consequences of anything done or omitted to be done by any such person in reliance, whether whole or partial, upon the whole or any part of the contents of this publication.

Contents

Chapter 1	Earning income as a young adult	1
Chapter 2	Spending, saving and investing	9
Chapter 3	The power of compound interest	15
Chapter 4	Saving and investing options	23
Chapter 5	The big financial goals	32
Chapter 6	Credit cards and high interest debt	39
Chapter 7	Building a budget	54
Chapter 8	Key paperwork	56
Chapter 9	Understanding tax	61
Chapter 10	Superannuation	68
Chapter 11	Buying a car	75
Chapter 12	Thinking about renting and moving out of home	82
Chapter 13	Philanthropy	88
Chapter 14	Gambling	94
Chapter 15	Experiences vs stuff	98
Chapter 16	Higher education loan programs	103

CHAPTER 1

Earning income as a young adult

"Any opportunity to be helpful is an opportunity to earn money"

– Chris Brogan

A note about opportunities to earn income

You often hear older people talking about the 'good old days'. However, I wonder if perhaps the 'good old days' of earning income as a young adult aren't with us right now. As I look around and see teenagers earning money from part-time work at food outlets and retail stores, from their own small businesses, from coaching and from their hobbies, it seems that there are more opportunities than ever for a motivated young adult to earn some money.

This first chapter in this book is about looking at the opportunities that exist to earn an income. We can't go through all the possibilities here. My hope is that by the end of the chapter you will have an idea of what other young people are doing to earn an income and, if you are keen to start earning, some places to look.

The basics

As a high school student teaching the subject Business, when we get to a class discussion about earning money, I am fascinated by the variety of ways students are doing it. Some earn money from doing chores at home, others by helping out in households close by – mowing lawns and babysitting are popular. Still others make money from their hobbies, for example, soccer players refereeing, swimmers teaching learn-to-swim classes and musicians taking classes for younger students. And there are always a few students who have started their own business, from selling items at the markets to online businesses selling specialised products.

Digging a little deeper

The Australian Institute of Family Studies (2017) did a survey that looked at the work habits of young Australians (aifs.gov.au/media/money-main-motivator-working-teens). It found that:

- Of young Australians aged 12 to 13, 16% were working an average of three hours per week earning $31 per week (adjusted for inflation, likely to be closer to $40 per week in 2023).
- Of young Australians aged 14 to 15, 39% were working an average of six hours per week earning $77 per week (adjusted for inflation, likely to be closer to $100 per week in 2023).

The survey mentioned a multitude of working opportunities that these 12- to 15-year-olds were involved with, including:

- Babysitting
- Sales assistant
- Checkout operator
- Waiter/waitress
- Labourer
- Kitchen hand
- Fast food cooks
- Helping in the family business
- Coaching sports (I suspect refereeing sport, too, although this was not mentioned)

And it acknowledged that people earning income in the 12- to 13-year age range tend to have more informal jobs, including jobs like babysitting, helping out with sports and working in the family business. One of the limitations to earning an income as a teenager is that different states have different rules around the age at which you can work for an employer, and different employers have different policies.

A great resource for information about working is the McDonald's website (McDonald's, 2023) under the FAQ (Frequently Asked Questions): 'What is the minimum age policy at McDonald's?'. At the time I looked at it, McDonald's was happy to employ people from age 14 if that met the laws in the state in which the person lived. The McDonald's website (https://careers.mcdonalds.com.au/faqs) had a great summary of the rules around age and working in each state.

A word about your reputation as a young adult

While we don't have the time to go into detail about the process of applying for a job, the key documents you will need to apply for a job with an employer – like McDonald's – will include a cover letter and resume. A little bit of research online will provide you with great examples of both, and you might even get some experience writing cover letters and resumes at school.

Your resume sets out your characteristics and experiences that make you suited to a position – which leads to a point I want to make. When you are given an opportunity to be involved in an activity – from sporting teams, musical teams, volunteering, academic activities like the ASX sharemarket game or an optional maths competition – I would suggest you do the activity and keep a record of what you have done.

These activities may not seem like a lot, but they show a variety of characteristics to a potential employer, including teamwork, leadership, interest in the wider world and concern for others. Every time you successfully participate in an extra activity, and keep a record of it, you are building your reputation as a young adult.

Stories of 'getting it done'

My favourite sport is basketball and, like many sports, they are crying out for referees. The basketball associate I am closest to often holds half-day referee training courses, before employing those who complete the training as referees. What is better than getting paid $15 to referee a 50-minute basketball game, being part of the sport you enjoy and getting a little exercise? Referee five games on a weekend morning and you go home with $75 from your morning's work. In the past few years, many basketball games have moved away from having volunteers (for example, parents) scoring the game to paying people to do this – it's another way to earn some money from participating in a game of sport.

I do some work as a part-time journalist, writing for an online magazine that publishes personal finance stories. This interest led me to notice three online journalists producing great-quality content: 'HER WAY', '6 News Australia' and 'CovidBaseAU'. They all had ways of supporting their work, through small, regular payments. The common elements in all three news sources, aside from their genuine quality, is that the people producing the journalism are all still at school. Not only are they all earning some money from the quality journalism they are creating, but they are also building their professional reputation, learning a lot with some extraordinary experiences. 6 News Australia has interviewed a variety of political leaders; HER WAY has done many amazing extended interviews with elite athletes; and *The Guardian* ran a great article on the surprise of people when they found out that "one of the most authoritative Covid-19 tracking sites [CovidBaseAU] in Australia is run by three teenagers".

A final word

Household chores. Employment. Refereeing. Coaching. Babysitting. Mowing lawns. Fast food. Retail. Starting your own micro-business. If you are interested in finding a way to earn an income, there are opportunities that you can investigate to build a plan to make it happen.

And, just like taking advantage of sporting, musical, volunteering and academic opportunities are ways of building your reputation as a young adult, so is successfully earning an income – the benefits go beyond just earning some money.

CHAPTER 2

Spending, saving and investing

"Annual income twenty pounds, annual expenditure nineteen and six, result happiness. Annual income twenty pounds, annual expenditure twenty pounds and six, result misery"

– Charles Dickens

A note about a key decision: Spending? Saving? Investing?

Since it was 1966 that we last had pounds as our currency in Australia, perhaps we should start by modernising this quote just a touch using decimal currency and a more modern version of what an annual income might be:

"Annual income $50,000, annual expenses $49,000, result happiness. Annual income $50,000, annual expenses $51,000, result misery."

Modernised or not, this has been a favourite quote of mine for some time, written by the renown 19th-century author Charles Dickens. What I did not realise, until recently, was that what had inspired him to write the quote was his father being thrown into jail for unpaid debts. Dickens had seen first-hand the trauma of spending more than you earn.

The idea behind this quote is where we start this book – when it comes to money, are you going to be a saver? A spender? Or a bit of both?

The basics

According to the website Growing up in Australia (growingup inaustralia.gov.au), half of Australian 16- to 17-year-olds are in a part-time job. In fact, from the age of 12–13, it reported students starting to work in paid employment. When you include students who might earn income from other ventures – for example, working for themselves babysitting, doing gardening, helping out in the family business – it is reasonable to say that most young adults will start earning an income during their high school years.

When you start earning, as the statistics suggest for most people during their high school years, you will start to build an important habit with your income:

- How much of each pay will you spend?
- Will you develop the habit of saving a little from each pay?
- Might you even develop the habit of investing a little from each pay?

Digging a little deeper

Spending. Saving. Investing. Let's start this section by looking at a definition for each of these terms.

- The idea of **'spending'** from each pay is straightforward – this is the money that is used each time you are paid. This is likely to be a mix of payments for necessities – for example, if you are paying some board to the adults at home or have to buy groceries or clothes – and lifestyle spending, for example, going to the movies or a concert.

- **Saving** is about medium-term needs – putting some money away each pay for future payments. This might be about regular bills, for example, having enough money set aside for the insurance and registration for your car, or for larger items you are looking for in the future, like buying a car or doing some travel.

- **Investing** is about the long term – putting a small amount of money away regularly into investments that (hopefully) will provide an attractive return over a long period of time. In Australia, superannuation is a compulsory saving scheme that will do a lot of the investing work for you, although many people will have some other investments alongside their superannuation, to help get ahead financially.

As a young adult, I would like to propose three unique elements of opportunity that you have as you think about what you are going to do (spending, saving and investing) with your money:

1. You get the chance to build habits – James Clear (2018), author of the bestselling book *Atomic Habits,* defines a habit as an "automatic response to a specific situation". A great chance to build habits is as you start out, in this case as you start out earning money – the habit (automatic response) of how you choose to allocate your pay (specific situation) is one that you can start early, and use to influence the way you manage your income over a lifetime.

2. You often have fewer costs for necessities if you are not living independently. For people living with adults (for example, parents, carers or family), they might be expected to contribute some 'board' once they are earning some income (board is a payment towards household costs), however, it is often less than the true cost of food, accommodation, electricity and internet that is provided. Without having to pay too much towards items like accommodation and food, it is a great chance to put a higher proportion of income towards saving and investing.

3. Starting to invest early gives you access to compounding interest over time – there is a whole chapter of compound interest next, however, the important executive summary is that the earlier you start investing, the greater the rewards.

A final word

There is perhaps nothing more profound than the difference between happiness and misery; and Dickens reminds us of the way money can impact us.

As a young adult, the decision between spending, saving and investing is an important one, both in terms of the results they give you financially, and also in terms of the financial habits that you are choosing for your future.

CHAPTER 3

The power of compound interest

"Compound interest is the most powerful force in the universe"

– Albert Einstein

A note about a powerful force – compound interest

Compound interest is a valuable concept to understand if you want a thorough understanding of how money works. It refers to the way savings and investments can increase their earnings over time. It also refers to the way a debt, for example, credit card debt, can rapidly increase if it is not paid off. The idea that compound interest works 'over time' is important – compound interest rewards those who are patient.

This is the focus of this chapter: what is compound interest, and why is it important?

The basics

I want to illustrate the way compound interest works by using an example. Let us say that you have saved $1,000, and you want to take it and deposit the $1,000 at the bank. Assuming the bank is paying 10% interest (a little higher than you can get as I write this in 2023, however, it is an easy calculation to do in your head), you will earn $100 in interest over a year and have $1,100 in your bank account.

Let's assume that for year 2, you leave that money there. In year 2, you will earn 10% interest on the $1,100 starting balance, or $110. Your ending balance will be $1,210.

In year 3, if you leave the funds in there, the 10% interest will amount to $121 and, by the end of the year, the balance will be $1,331.

This in itself doesn't seem exciting, however, the impact over long periods of time is significant. The table on the next page sets out what is happening every five years from the first to the 40th year of having $1,000 set aside, without it being touched, earning 10% per annum.

This illustrates the power of compound interest – as more and more interest is reinvested (kept) in the account, to earn interest in the following year, the interest earnt each year increases more and more quickly, as does the ending balance of the $1,000.

Some of you might have come across an old quiz show called *Who Wants to be a Millionaire?*. The show isn't relevant here, however, the question is. If you started with $1,000 and placed it into an investment earning 10% each year, it would take 73 years to turn that $1,000 into a million dollars. That seems like an impressive feat.

Interest earned and account balance over time for $1,000 earning 10% annually (assuming no withdrawals)

	Interest earned in the year	Ending balance of original $1,000 deposit
Year 1	$100	$1,100
Year 5	$146	$1,610
Year 10	$236	$2,594
Year 15	$380	$4,177
Year 20	$612	$6,727
Year 25	$984	$10,834
Year 30	$1586	$17,449
Year 35	$2,554	$28,102
Year 40	$4,114	$45,259

Digging a little deeper – and a dose of reality

Now, let's add a little touch of reality to the thought that we can stash away $1,000 today and become a millionaire down the track with no other work.

Firstly, a million dollars in 73 years sounds impressive, and indeed it is impressive, however, it won't buy as much as a million dollars does today because inflation tends to push the price of goods and services up over time.

Secondly, there is no investment that is going to pay us interest or investment earnings at a steady rate of 10% per annum. There are options, such as share investments and property investments, both of which we will touch upon later in the book, that provide an average return of around 10% per annum, however, returns from the sharemarket are volatile; they might be 20% in one year and –5% the next, and it is impossible to find a slice of property that you can buy for $1,000. So, the 10% per annum assumption is challenging in reality.

That said, the greatest opportunity for young investors to experience compound interest over a lifetime is superannuation. This is a scheme where your employer deposits a little over 10% of your income into an investment account that is then invested and grows in value until you retire. A chapter later in the book looks specifically at superannuation, an exciting opportunity for you to get compound interest working for you.

The importance of patience

In the example used to illustrate compound interest, we saw an initial investment of $1,000 earning $100 a year turn into a final balance after 40 years of just over $45,000, earning more than $4,000 per year.

Here is a huge challenge in reality – setting aside and leaving an investment for years is a big ask. The early years didn't see any exciting increase in income earned, $100 first, then $110, then $121…

Compounding interest requires patience as an important ingredient.

The bad side of compound interest – a debt that keeps growing

Albert Einstein, the renowned scientist whose quote starts this chapter, has another important point:

> *"Compound interest is the eighth wonder of the world. He who understands it, earns it; he who doesn't, pays it."*

While the 'earning' side of compound interest can be exciting, there is a darker side – which happens to people who borrow money and are unable to pay the interest back. That interest earns interest in the second year, increasing the debt at an increasing rate. And, while we have used 10% as an example of how someone might earn an attractive rate, borrowing rates can be much higher, pushing credit card debt up more quickly. For example, a credit card often has interest rates of around 20%, increasing the size of the debt and the extra interest very quickly.

A final word

Investment opportunities, and the opportunity to borrow money, are a significant element in the money landscape.

Understanding the power of compound interest gives you some thoughts on:

- How you might avoid paying compound interest by avoiding debts like personal loans and credit cards.
- How you might utilise compound interest as part of a saving and investing strategy.
- The importance of patience in allowing compound interest to work.

Most of all, as a young adult, being aware of the way compound interest works over time might let you see what a unique position you are in to start early, and get compound interest working in your favour.

CHAPTER 4

Saving and investing options

"Do not save what is left after spending.
Spend what is left after saving"

– Warren Buffett (famous investor and billionaire)

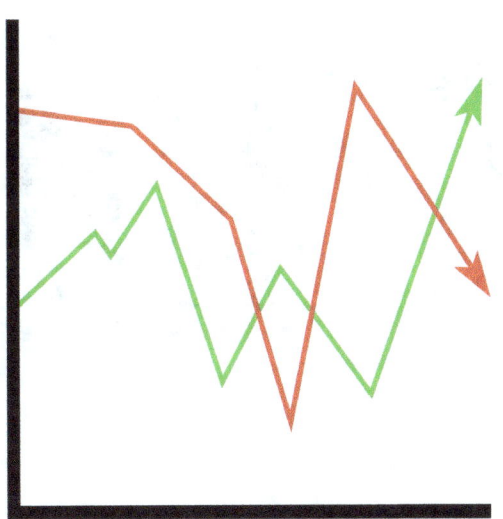

A note about options for saving and investing

Previously in this book we introduced the three options that exist when some money is earnt:

- Spend it
- Save it
- Invest it (for the long term)

This chapater looks to provide some more details around the 'how' of savings, and the 'how' of investing.

The basics

When you earn money, it will be up to you how much you choose to spend, how much you choose to save and how much you choose to invest.

That said, a benchmark for someone in their high school years, who has most of their living costs (food, accommodation) provided for them, might be to spend 60% of what they earn, save 30% and invest 10% – and let's be clear from the start, only the most financially engaged people will start by setting aside a regular amount to invest.

An important principle here is that of 'paying yourself first' – that is, putting the money that you want to save and invest (if you choose to) away as soon as you are paid, and then spending the remainder of the money.

Digging a little deeper

A 60% spending, 30% saving and 10% investing split has been proposed as a starting point – however, you will need to decide on your own split. Some people will be comfortable spending 100% of their money. Others might try to save and invest the majority of what they earn, particularly if they have a goal in mind (perhaps buying a car).

Remember what each of these three categories are for:

- **Spending** is about the choices you make for spending your money from week to week, from movies to playing sports to new clothes.

- **Saving** is the money set aside for medium-term goals – the bigger items that you want to buy, such as a new phone, a car or travel.

- **Investing** is the money set aside for the very long term – more than 10 years down the track. Regularly setting aside a modest portion of your income for long-term investing will appeal to some financially ambitious people.

Saving

If you want to earn income, you are going to need a bank account. Most people will benefit from having two connected bank accounts:

1. A low-fee transaction account that allows you to have money deposited into it and allows you to withdraw money.
2. A linked online savings account that allows you to transfer money into it, where it earns a high rate of interest.

I would suggest that as you are thinking about setting up bank accounts, you pop into a bank branch at the local shopping centre and ask two important questions:

1. "What bank accounts do you offer that I could I use for a low-fee transaction account that could also link to an online savings account with a higher interest rate?"
2. "What identity documents do I need to need to open these accounts?"

Make sure that you also find out about any fees, and the interest rate on the higher interest rate/online savings account. Once you have the answer to these questions, compare what your local bank branch has suggested with some online research into what else is available.

The second step, hopefully with the help of the adults at home, is to put together the identity documents (perhaps birth certificates and Medicare card) you need to open the accounts.

Once you have set up a low-fee transaction account and online savings account, you have everything you need.

Before moving on, I want to throw in another Warren Buffett quote, as he is a successful saver and investor who started young and amassed billions. In a speech to college students, he said:

> *"The biggest mistake is not learning the habit of saving properly."*

That is my first challenge to you – will you make the effort to learn the habit of 'saving properly' as you start earning income?

Investing

If I was writing this note five years ago, I don't think I would have even talked about long-term investments for people aged 20 or under who are starting on their financial journey.

Two key reasons as to why investing under the age of 18 has been challenging are:

1. There are complexities with tax – if you earn more than $417 in earnings and are under the age of 18, the amount of earnings over $417 is taxed at the very high rate of 66%.
2. Investing has usually required largish minimum investment amounts, often thousands of dollars or more.

However, there has been a new group of investment options called 'micro-investments'. As I write in mid-2023, there are a number available in the Australian marketplace.

These allow people to make very small investments of money – even $5 at a time – into portfolios that include investment assets like Australian and overseas shares. Shares allow you to own parts of companies – benefitting from the earnings of their business. The important element to owning shares is that, while over long periods of time they have had higher returns for investors, they are also volatile and can fall sharply in value.

I use the micro-investing app Raiz, and for those interested in investing, it might be a good place to get started. I use the 'moderate' portfolio (you have a choice of portfolios you can invest in), and it includes about 50% invested in shares (including overseas and Australian shares), and 50% invested in cash-like investments.

Investing is not easy – the volatility (ups and downs) of markets is challenging – which is another reason that only using 10% of your income for long-term investing in volatile assets like shares, as you learn about the realities of investing, makes sense.

However (and I hate writing this!), there are still limitations on people under the age of 18 opening investment accounts. My suspicion is that the best way if you are under 18 years of age might be to ask an adult at home to open an account in their name that you contribute to initially.

An investment approach that works

In this chapter we have looked at the idea of saving and investing.

I want to introduce an investing approach that is low cost, simple and reliable. It is worth keeping in mind when you get to a stage in your money journey that you want to start building an investment portfolio.

The approach that I want to introduce you to is 'index investing'.

When we listen, read or watch the news, we might come across a statement like, 'the ASX300 index rose by 1% today'. The ASX300 index calculates the average movement in price of the biggest 300 shares (companies) on the Australian sharemarket (names like BHP, Commonwealth Bank, Woolworths and CSL).

An index fund is an investment that allows you to invest in all of the companies in an index, for example, an index fund based on the ASX300 invests in the largest 300 companies in the Australian sharemarket. As an investor, you receive the average return in the market, less a small amount of costs.

There are any number of reasons that this investment approach works well, including that index funds are simple investments, they are well diversified (they give you exposure to a broad range of investments), they are low cost and they tend not to do too much trading, which in turn makes them reasonably tax efficient.

Let's have a look at how well index funds have provided returns for investors. As I write this in the second half of 2023, if I had invested $10,000 into an ASX300 index fund 10 years ago, it would have turned into $22,049 over that 10-year period. If I had invested $10,000 into a global index fund (based on the MSCI world index), over 10 years that amount would have grown to $32,079 (returns are to the end of August 2023). Both of these figures assume that you choose to reinvest your distributions from the funds. As an investor, it might make sense to have some of your money in Australian shares, and some in global shares.

A word of warning – as good as these returns seem at face value, it is worth remembering that investing in shares comes with volatility. For example, at the start of 2020 when Covid-19 was making an impact on the world, shares in Australia fell by around 40%.

In the Australian market, Vanguard is a large provider of index products and has some interesting material about index investing, as well as historical data in its 'digital index chart'. It might be a place to start when you are considering more information.

There have been whole books written about index investing, so this part of a chapter can only be a short introduction. However, when it comes time to set up an investment portfolio, index investing is worth considering as a simple, reliable, well-diversified (you get exposure to a wide range of underlying companies in each index that you invest in) and low-cost approach to investing.

A final word

This is a chapter that could have been a whole book.

Opening a transaction account and online savings account will take some effort, but it is an important financial step.

Starting an investment plan, perhaps using micro-investing, will allow you to learn about the reality of how investments work while moving towards long-term financial goals.

CHAPTER 5

The big financial goals

"Setting goals is the first step in turning the invisible into the visible"

– Tony Robbins (author and motivational speaker)

A note about financial goals

If you are earning some income, and have set up bank accounts that are working, you are ready to set and work towards some financial goals.

The most common financial goal I see high school students working towards is buying a car, and the second most common is saving to travel. This chapter looks at what you might do if you have a larger financial goal, like a car or travel, in mind.

The basics

This chapter revolves around common sense.

The core steps that we are going to discuss in terms of working towards a larger financial goal are:

- Take the time to know what you are working towards – a specific goal.
- Break the goal into smaller steps.
- Acknowledge and enjoy your progress along the way.

Digging a little deeper

Let's start with a common goal – a person who starts work at McDonald's at the age of 14 decides that one of the key things they would like to do with their money is buy a car when they turn 17. Let's give the person a name, Chloe.

This is a very reasonable goal for Chloe, so let's see how she goes about it.

The first step is to make the goal specific. This will require a little research to decide what sort of car might be of interest, and the price. Let's say, after a little research, Chloe decides that a 10-year-old hatchback is the aim, currently costing around $9,000.

Chloe has started to make the goal specific. Allowing for the car to be a little more expensive in three years' time, the final goal might be to have $10,000 saved in three years' time to buy a new (second-hand) car.

The second step is to break the goal into smaller steps: weeks, fortnights or months. In this case, Chloe decides to use months. She knows that there are 36 months in three years. That means she has to aim to save $10,000 ÷ 36 = $278 per month. Let's say Chloe is earning $125 per week, which will be $541 per month – effectively, if Chloe wants the car, she has to commit to saving about half of what she earns.

Two factors might help Chloe's progress towards this goal. The first is that over the holidays there is often the chance to work more hours and earn more money – if she continues to save 50% of her income while she is earning a little more, she has the chance to get ahead on her goal.

The second factor is that as she gets older, she is likely to be paid more. If Chloe keeps saving 50% of her income, she is also likely to get ahead a little as her pay increases.

Smaller steps and acknowledging progress

Now that Chloe knows she has to save $278 per month, she can start to track her progress. Setting up a notebook or Excel spreadsheet with the aim every month – so she can compare her actual progress to where she plans to be – will be a great way of seeing how Chloe is progressing with each of her monthly steps.

Chloe might even decide when she gets to each $1,000 milestone that she is going to celebrate her progress – perhaps allowing herself a favourite activity, like a night out at the movies or buying a new book.

We should note that we are assuming that Chloe has set up a transaction account and online savings account. At a practical level, what she will be doing, after each pay, is transferring the appropriate amount from her transaction account, which is where her pay will come in, through to her online savings account where it can build up, with a little interest earned, until the time she buys her car.

SMART goals

SMART goals are a way of organising thinking around a goal. The SMART model suggests that you may be more successful towards your goal if the thinking around that goal is:

- **S**pecific
- **M**easurable
- **A**chievable through actions
- **R**ealistic, and with a
- **T**imeframe

If we were to put Chloe's thinking about goals into a SMART goal format, it might look like this:

Specific (and written down)	Buy a $10,000 car at the age of 17. Set up a spreadsheet to write down the goal and track it.
Measurable	Every month save around $278.
Achievable through actions	Work part-time and save 50% of the income earned.
Realistic	It will be a challenge to do this over three years, however, it is possible.
Timeframe	A clear timeframe of three years, with celebrations along the way every time an extra $1,000 is saved.

A final word

While a lot of this chapter is common sense, it is worth taking the time to acknowledge that there are a couple of very important habits that are built by setting and working towards a financial goal.

The first is around the use of goals. Any time that we set and work towards a goal, we are building the skill of working towards an aim over time.

The second is a financial habit. If we want something, we are prepared to set out a plan to work towards it and stick with that plan.

If you have a significant financial goal, write it down, do some research to understand the cost, break it up into easy steps, record and celebrate your progress. A SMART goal might help you do this.

CHAPTER 6

Credit cards and high interest debt

"Credit card interest payments are the dumbest money of all"

– Hill Harper (author)

A note about credit cards and high interest debt

This chapter is about a financial stumble that people make – using a credit card to make purchases, then being unable to pay off the debt while being charged extremely high interest rates. The added expense of extra credit card payments and interest can cause financial stress.

We have already looked at compound interest, and the way an amount of money can increase over time – this chapter is largely about thinking carefully about the damage credit cards and high interest debts (personal loans, buy now pay later offers, payday advances) can do to a person financially.

The basics

19.94%.

According to Amanda Smith, writing an article for nerdwallet.com in 2022 (nerdwallet.com/aucredit-cards/how-do-credit-card-interest-rates-work), the average interest rate for credit card debt at the time was 19.94%. Not only that, for most credit cards interest will be added each month, so the following month not only will more interest be charged, it will also be charged on the previous months' interest, too… compounding interest working against you every month!

Put simply – no one with a reasonable job and decent financial knowledge should ever pay interest at the rate of 19.94%. *Ever.*

To put the figure of 19.94% in perspective, the cost of interest on a home loan at the time was around 5% and a car loan around 8%.

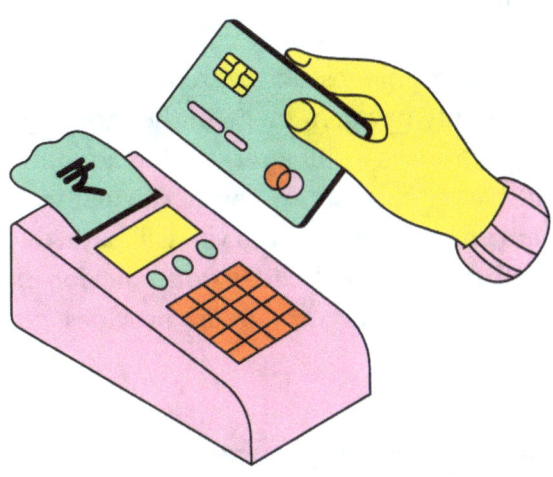

Digging a little deeper

To put some real-life figures around credit card interest – let's say someone uses a credit card with a 20% interest rate to pay for a $15,000 overseas holiday. When they return from the holiday, not only will they (hopefully) have some great memories, they will also have a $15,000 credit card debt.

Let's go to the credit card calculator at moneysmart.gov.au (an Australian Government website) to see how that works in reality.

The first important element we come across is the 'minimum monthly repayment' trick, where the bank that issues the credit card only requires a monthly repayment slightly above the level of the interest – so, effectively, the debt goes down very, very slowly and the bank makes *lots* of money (perhaps you are starting to wonder whether a credit card works best for a bank or for the person with the credit card!).

If your bank has a minimum monthly payment of 2% of the outstanding balance each month (which is not hypothetical – it is exactly what my bank charges on its credit cards) *and* you make the minimum monthly payment of 2% of the monthly balance (so, starting at $300 per month – still a reasonable amount of money to find each month), the moneysmart.gov.au calculator tells you it will take you **70 years and six months**, and you will pay a total of **$79,800** before paying off the $15,000 holiday you paid for using a credit card. (As an aside, moneysmart.gov.au provides great financial information and tools.)

Of course, most people will make higher than the minimum repayments. However, even if you were to pay $500 a month on repayments, it will take you three years and five months to pay off that holiday, and in the process, you will pay $20,475.

That holiday, that you have already enjoyed, will be taking $500 per month out of your pocket for the next 1,277 days… Or, to put it another way, the first $115 you earn every week, for 182 weeks, will go towards getting rid of that credit card debt.

This is the point at the heart of this chapter about credit cards and consumer debt – you are far better off financially avoiding them.

Credit card debt is not the only high-interest financial product that allows you to 'buy now and pay later' – a phrase that you should always be wary of. Some products, like the currently popular Afterpay that allows you to buy now and pay later, promote that they do not charge interest. Instead, they add late fees that are (according to Afterpay's website) "capped at 25% of the original order value". While it might not be called 'interest', a 25% late fee, much like a 20% credit card interest rate, is something that no one should pay.

The dishonesty of debt

Many years ago, I came across a perspective on credit card debts and loans generally while watching a TV interview. The financial expert said, "debt was dishonesty".

Let me explain what they meant with an example. Let's say you are out shopping for a jumper and are old enough that you have a credit card (you can't get a credit card until the age of 18). You also have $50 cash that you have set aside to spend on your jumper. You see a nice $50 jumper. However, you also see a brand name jumper for $125. Your choice – buy the $50 jumper with cash, or buy the $125 jumper and put $75 on a credit card?

The 'dishonesty', according to the finance expert, is buying the $125 jumper. If you buy the $50 jumper it is not dishonesty, it is what you can afford. However, if you buy the $125 jumper, you are pretending to be someone who can afford that jumper – and in reality, you cannot. You are using some debt, the dishonesty in this instance, to help you buy the jumper.

The honest way to buy the $125 jumper is to work a few more hours and save a little longer and pay for it using your money.

Dishonesty using debt, according to the expert, could be seen in people borrowing money for expensive cars, expensive holidays and luxury items – but rather than paying for it with money they have, they are using debt which, as we know, will have to be paid back later, with interest.

The focus of this chapter has been avoiding paying high interest rates on debt. Some people *do* use credit cards to put their transactions on each month and pay the card off so they do not pay any interest – and this can be a way to use a credit card as a financial tool. That said, a debit card linked to your bank account can do exactly the same thing, with no risk of running up debt, and is my preference.

A final word

In general terms, it is hard to get access to credit card debt, and other consumer debt, until you are 18 years old – if you are younger than 18, this chapter highlights a future pitfall that is worth avoiding.

Regardless of age, if you make a promise to yourself to never flirt with paying high interest rates on consumer debt, you are likely to live a happier life than if you find yourself in debt and paying part of every pay that you earn in interest.

CHAPTER 7

Building a budget

"Those who buy what they do not need,
steal from themselves"

– **Swedish proverb**

A note about budgeting

In Year 8 Economics we learn about the 'economic problem', which is that there are unlimited wants and limited resources. This is profoundly important at all levels of economics, including at a personal level – unfortunately, we are not going to have enough for all of our wants.

Budgeting is a process that allows us to be thoughtful about how we spend our 'limited resources'.

The basics

A budget does not have to be complex to be effective, nor does it have to be rigidly stuck to. The aim of doing a budget is to identify how much you can save each week and set that money aside while enjoying the money you have to spend. Spending 20 minutes with a piece of paper or a computer should allow you to identify how much you are spending and how much you are saving.

Like many financial habits, if you start early in thinking about the process of budgeting, you are building a useful habit. At high school a budget will likely not be as complex as once you have moved out of home and are working, studying at university or completing an apprenticeship – but starting with a simple budget builds a habit to build on later.

Digging a little deeper

To get started with the habit of budgeting, you need to choose whether to prepare a weekly, fortnightly, monthly or even annual budget. If you are uncertain, I would suggest a monthly budget – it allows you to track what is happening over a number of weeks, so if your income fluctuates from week to week, over a month you should see a reasonable approximation of what you earn.

The Government website **moneysmart.gov.au** suggests a five-step process to budgeting, which we will work through one step at a time, and then set up a budgeting template that you might use to start building your own budget.

Step 1: Record your income

The first step is to record your income. As we go, let's use the example of Charlie, a Year 10 student who earns, on average, $120 a week from a part-time job while also mowing three people's lawns for $35 each. Charlie will have:

$$\$120 \times 4.5 \text{ (assuming 4.5 weeks in a month)} + \$35 \times 3$$
$$= \$645 \text{ in income for the month.}$$

Step 2: Add up expenses

Expenses are regular 'needs', or essential items that have to be paid for. If you are living at home, it may be that your parents or carers are covering a significant proportion of this amount.

Charlie's key expenses are $40 per month for a mobile phone and $20 per week that he pays in board. In this case Charlie's expenses will be:

$$\$20 \times 4.5 + \$40 = \$130$$

Step 3: 'Pay yourself first' – set a savings goal

This is setting aside the money for your saving goal *before* your day-to-day spending.

Let's say that Charlie is saving up for a holiday at the end of Year 12 and has identified that he needs to set aside $100 per month for his long-term savings in his online savings account. Charlie is also keen on building some investments and sets aside $50 per month to put towards his balanced investment in a Raiz that his mum has opened for him.

In total, he has savings and investments of $150 per month.

Step 4: Identify your spending limits

Charlie is starting to put together some key information about his situation:

- He earns $645 per month.
- He has 'needs' (expenses) of $130 per month.
- He will set aside saving/investment amounts of $150 per month.

That leaves him $365, or about $80 per week, for his 'wants' – for example, eating out, hobbies and entertainment.

Step 5: Adjust your budget

There are a lot of circumstances that Charlie might find changing over time – his level of income, his saving and investing goals, or the amount he finds himself spending on wants. At any time, his budget can be adjusted.

However, if he is saving his $100 in his online bank account, and $50 in his Raiz account and coping with the $80 per week spending on 'wants', then there is little need to keep thinking too much about the budget – everything is working nicely.

You can use the following template to develop a budget; on the left are the five headings. In the column on the right, jot down all the items that fit, and then come to a total at the bottom of each section (if you are a little computer savvy, setting up a spreadsheet is a great way of doing a budget).

Income
(from a job, working for others, pocket money/chores)

Expenses
('needs' including board, mobile phone)

Saving and investing goal
(pay yourself first)

Saving goal:

Investing goal:

Total savings:

Spending limits
('wants' including entertainment, eating out, hobbies)

Checking it adds up:

Total income:

Less

Total expenses:

Total savings:

Total spending:

Surplus/deficit:

(If there is a significant deficit or surplus, you should go back and check what adjustments you are prepared to make to expenses, savings and spending.)

The next step – a bills account

The first time a person is likely to outgrow the model of the budget we have looked at is when they first own a car. This is because a car brings a series of ongoing expenses including registration, insurance and repairs. These can often be big expenses, and if they come at the same time, as insurance and registration often does, it can be a significant amount of cash to find.

This is where a second online savings account might be useful. Making regular deposits into the account means that when bills are due, the money is already saved.

Let's say that Charlie buys a car and calculates that the bills associated with the car will be $2,400 per year (insurance, registration and repairs). That comes to $200 per month, and by opening a 'bills account', he can set aside $200 a month so that when the insurance, registration and repairs need to be paid, he has money set aside.

As an aside, he will struggle to do that on his current income of $645 per month, so he might have to take on extra hours at work to be able to afford the extra expense of a car.

A final word

Setting up a budget is a great process to go through to assess where you are financially, and whether you are able to set aside some funds for your saving and investing ambitions.

While it is common sense, it becomes a useful money habit. After all, there is a reason businesses and large organisations all work to a budget – budgets are a useful tool in understanding and managing the flow of money in and out.

CHAPTER 8

Key paperwork

"I have so much paperwork.
I'm afraid my paperwork has paperwork"

– Gabrielle Zevin (author)

A note about the paperwork you will meet on the start of your financial journey

Part of the reality of being a young adult, particularly if you have a job, is that suddenly you are a financial entity. Suddenly, you need to organise and manage important paperwork.

The basics

This chapter contains what I think are the six 'moments' of paperwork that are most important as you start earning an income. They are:

1. Opening a bank account
2. Getting a tax file number
3. Filling out a tax file number declaration (at each new job)
4. Your superannuation records
5. Understanding income tax and MyGov
6. Keeping an up-to-date resume

The adults at home are likely to be able to give you some more information on each of these, so have a chat with them about what I have included here, as it is just a starting point.

Digging a little deeper

Let's look at each of these:

1. Opening a bank account

If you are going to have a job, your employer will need a bank account to pay your income into. Chapter 4 includes more detail about opening a transaction account and online savings account. The process to research and open an account, and provide the identity documents you need, might take a week or two.

2. Getting a tax file number

A tax file number is a unique number that identifies you to the Australian Taxation Office (ATO). It is likely that once you start working for an employee, you will need a tax file number.

The ATO is the place to go to apply for your tax file number. As we hinted at with opening a bank account, there are also documents that the ATO will require in processing your application for a tax file number that you will need to organise. The ATO website is the best resource to understand the steps in completing the form to get your tax file number (See ATO.gov.au).

3. Filling out a tax file number declaration (at each new job)

When you start working at a new job, your employer will have some paperwork that they require you to complete. This will likely include a tax file number declaration form. This lets the employer (your boss) know that you have a tax file number, and what it is. There is one important question on the form, along the lines of 'do you want to claim the tax-free threshold from this payer?'. The tax-free threshold refers to the fact that in Australia you can earn $18,200 per year and pay no income tax. Assuming you only have one job you should answer YES.

4. Your superannuation records

If you are under 18, you are only required to be paid superannuation if you work more than 30 hours a week. Some employers also pay superannuation to workers under the age of 18 even though they don't have to.

Once you turn 18, and are working, you are highly likely to be receiving some superannuation. There is a whole note on superannuation later in this book – in short, it is a retirement savings scheme that employers have to contribute to.

As soon as you start receiving contributions, you can track your superannuation account – you will be able to set up log-in details, so you can watch your superannuation account.

When you change jobs, in most cases you can ask your employer to keep contributing to your existing superannuation fund, if you are happy with the fund. This is a great strategy to keep your superannuation in one place, and growing over time.

5. Understanding income tax and MyGov

It is likely that once you start working, you will also have to complete an annual income tax return. This lets the tax office know how much you have earned, how much your employer has taken out of your pay in tax, any deductions you have (for example, charitable contributions). The ATO will then calculate the amount of tax owing, or owing to you.

My.gov.au is an online portal where you can complete your tax return. The benefit of using this portal is that generally it has all your financial information, for example, the income you have earned and any bank interest, automatically uploaded about a month or two after the end of the financial year (the financial year in Australia ends on 30 June). You only need to check this information, add any other information (for example, any deductions to charitable donations) to complete your income tax.

You will need to go to my.gov.au to create an account.

6. Keeping an up-to-date resume

A resume is a summary of your professional experience, knowledge, skills and achievements. There are great examples online – search 'resume tips for high school students' as a starting point. Best practice is to continually update your resume as you have new experiences, opportunities and achievements.

Consider the following:

- You enter a maths competition at school and win a distinction certificate.
- You act as manager for shifts at your work.
- You volunteer over the holidays.

These examples show an employer the sort of person you are. Update your resume to include these as they happen, so it presents the best version of yourself when you apply for positions in the future.

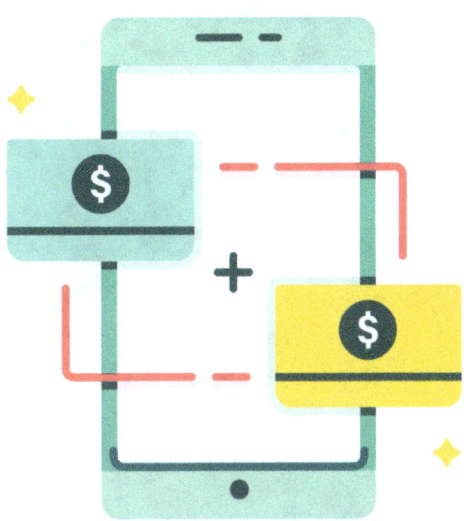

A final word

Paperwork is not fun, but it is an important element of your money journey. You might need some help from an adult to get started, however, if you can get these six key items organised, then you are well on your way.

CHAPTER 9

Understanding tax

"Paying tax is not a punishment.
It's a responsibility"

– Chris Matthews (author)

A note about three common taxes you will encounter

One of the realities in life is paying tax. The aim of this note is to introduce three key taxes: income tax, goods and services tax (GST) and capital gains tax, so that you have an understanding of each, given these are the three taxes likely to impact you over time.

The basics

Income tax is the tax we pay on our earnings from work and investments, and is likely to be the largest value tax that you pay each year. Generally, your employer takes tax out of your income each pay, and after the end of the financial year (30 June), you submit a tax return to pay any extra owing, or receive a refund if you have paid more than needed.

GST is a 10% tax that is paid on most items that you buy. For example, if you pay $7.70 for a burger, 70 cents of this is tax that is collected by the business and paid to the Government.

Capital gains tax is the tax you pay if you sell an investment that has gone up in value.

Digging a little deeper

Income tax

The following table from the ATO sets out the income tax rates for the 2023 financial year – and even if the rates change in future years, the understanding of how they work is likely to stay the same.

Resident tax rates 2022–23

Taxable income	Tax on this income
0 – $18,200	Nil
$18,201 – $45,000	19 cents for each $1 over $18,200
$45,001 – $120,000	$5,092 plus 32.5 cents for each $1 over $45,000
$120,001 – $180,000	$29,467 plus 37 cents for each $1 over $120,000
$180,001 and over	$51,667 plus 45 cents for each $1 over $180,000

The first row under the headings sets out that if you earn up to $18,200, you pay no income tax. That is likely to be a common situation for people doing some part-time work through university or high school. There may be some weeks or fortnights where you have worked an unusually large number of hours, and your employer has taken some tax out of your pay. However, if you end up earning less than $18,200 for the year, you will not have to pay any tax and you will receive a tax refund of any tax paid. This will happen after you put in your income tax return.

The second row shows what happens to the amount of income earned above $18,200. It is taxed at 19% (this is what is meant in the table when it says 19 cents for each $1). Importantly, you still pay no tax on the first $18,200 you earn and, on amounts above this (up to $45,000), you pay tax at the rate of 19%.

For example, let's assume that Olive earns $35,000 from her work (it is a reasonable sum of money, because Olive tends to work close to full-time over the holidays). She doesn't pay any income tax on the first $18,200. She earns $16,800 that she has to pay tax on at the rate of 19% ($35,000 – $18,200 = $16,800), so Olive will pay $16,800 × 19% = $3,192 in income tax.

Let's take this one step further. At tax time, Olive finds that as well as earning $35,000, her employer has taken out $4,292 in tax over the year. When she submits her tax return for the year, the calculation will show that she has paid $1,100 more tax than is needed ($4,292 – $3,192), and she will receive a $1,100 tax refund. Receiving a tax refund is common particularly when, like Olive, you have worked uneven hours over the year.

Finally, there is also a 2% Medicare levy that is paid on your income – used to support Government-provided medical services.

GST

GST is a 10% tax paid on most of the goods and services that you purchase. When you dine out, go to the movies or buy new clothes, 10% of what you spend is GST. The GST is collected by the business selling the goods or services, and passed on to the Government, usually every three months.

Next time you go shopping, have a look at the receipts and you will see the GST on the items you have purchased.

Capital gains tax

Let's say, as an investor, you buy some shares for $1,000 and then sell them for $1,500. You have made a gain on the shares of $500 – this is called your capital gain and is added to your income to be taxed.

However, there is a rule that allows a 50% discount for capital gains tax if you hold an investment for more than 12 months. The shares in this example were owned for two years, so the $500 gain would be discounted to $250 and added to your income.

A word on your mindset towards tax

I had a grandfather who was an accountant. His attitude towards tax was that he did not mind paying tax, because it meant he had made money.

Some years ago, I travelled to Cambodia. It is a developing country with significant poverty. Not many people would pay much tax – and equally, Government services like healthcare, social security and education were well below what we have in Australia. It made me think that my contribution of tax led to some tremendous benefits for me in Australia – everything from quality healthcare to great roads to social security to education – and beyond.

A lot of people don't like the idea of paying tax, however, if you link the payment of tax to the opportunity you have had to earn income, and the services that come from paying tax, perhaps you might find it an easier 'price to pay'.

A final word

In one short chapter we can only touch on the basics of income tax (and the Medicare levy), GST and capital gains tax.

However, if you understand these basics of income tax, GST and capital gains tax, you have a working knowledge of three common taxes that are likely to impact you as you earn, invest and spend money.

CHAPTER 10
Superannuation

"If you want to save, put money into superannuation. You will never find a better savings vehicle"

– Peter Costello (former Australian treasurer)

A note about superannuation

Superannuation is a topic that involves the 'future you'. It is a great way to save money over a lifetime, and the sooner you take some interest in your superannuation, the sooner it becomes a useful part of your financial situation.

The basics

Superannuation is where your employer contributes a percentage of the income you earn into a low-tax savings scheme that is set up to fund your retirement. The current rate employers have to contribute at is 11%, rising to 12% by mid-2025.

Show me the money... (or how to be a millionaire)

I want to start by giving you a sense of the possible value of superannuation over a working lifetime. Assuming that you work from age 22 to age 62, earning an average wage, having just the compulsory 11% of employer contributions made for you (less the 15% contributions tax that is taken by the Government from each contribution) in a fund that earns 5% more than inflation – at age 62 you will have $1.037 million dollars in today's money.

Superannuation is likely to be a significant asset for you.

The challenge of superannuation

The challenge for a young person thinking superannuation is that it is very much a 'future you' concept. The rules of superannuation say that, except in situations of serious hardship, you can't access the money until you are 60 years old. That is a long way away!

However, your 60-year-old self is going to appreciate your younger self if you:

- Understand how superannuation works.
- Keep track of your superannuation (as people change jobs, or move houses, many lose track of superannuation amounts they have earned).
- Keep your superannuation in one place, so that you pay less in fees.
- Take a little time to choose an investment option that makes sense (generally a low-fee growth or balanced investment option).

Understanding how superannuation works

Superannuation in one sentence: *Your employer has to pay 11% of your income into your superannuation account, that you can then use when you turn 60 to fund your retirement.*

If you are reading this and are under the age of 18, you are entitled to superannuation payments if you work 30 hours or more a week. Over the age of 18, you should receive contributions.

It is likely that your employer will help you set up your superannuation account, and from there it should work like a bank account. You should receive some details in the post, be able to set up online access to watch the account balance grow and even make decisions about which investment option to choose.

It is your money – don't be shy about contacting your superannuation fund if you have any questions.

Keeping track of your superannuation

Around $13.8 billion is lost superannuation in Australia – this is superannuation that has gone astray from its owner when people have moved or changed jobs.

The majority of employers now offer 'choice of superannuation'. If you start a new job, this should allow you to receive contributions from your new employer into any existing superannuation fund that you have. As you move from one job to the next, as most people do over time, trying to keep all your superannuation in the one is a great strategy. If you have two jobs, there is no reason both employers can't be contributing into your one superannuation account. This leads to an important benefit of having one account: keeping fees lower.

One account – lower fees

Superannuation accounts have a variety of fees. My own superannuation is with Australian Super. It charges an administration fee of $1 per week. This is not huge, however, if you have three superannuation accounts you would be paying an extra $2 per week – or $104 a year – more in fees than needed.

Understanding the investment option

I could write a whole book on investment options for superannuation.

The most important element is: this investment options are a trade-off between return and volatility (the extent to which your superannuation balance will go up and down in value as markets move).

You can choose a low return in a cash account. There will be almost no volatility, but returns are likely to be the lowest. As I write this in 2023, the 10-year return for cash in the Australian Super cash account has been 1.76% per annum.

Over the long run, a balanced investment option is ideal for a lot of people – this has a balance of investments including some cash, property and both Australian and international shares. The 10-year return for this investment with Australian Super as I write has been 9.32% per annum over 10 years.

There is an argument that as you start out with superannuation, you can afford to have more volatility, ups and downs, and should invest in a growth option. The return for this fund with Australian Super has been 10.28% per annum over the past 10 years.

The most important idea to remember is that, as investors, we tend to be terrible at picking the ups and downs of markets – we are best to choose the investment option we want and stick with it, accepting there will be ups and downs over time.

A final word

I have worked with people and investments for some years. I have never come across someone around the age of 60, who is retiring, saying, "I wish I had a bit less superannuation".

Superannuation is also likely to be one of your most significant assets, and paying attention to get the most out of it is an idea worth thinking about.

CHAPTER 11

Buying a car

"If you buy a $28,000 car, in four years it will be worth about 11,000 bucks"

– Dave Ramsey (financial author)

A note about buying a car

Buying a car is a unique financial decision. It is likely to be the most expensive item that you buy that falls in value. As such, it is worth being thoughtful about your decision to buy a car, should you choose to buy one.

The basics

There are two points about car ownership that are useful to recognise as a young adult, and these are the focus of this chapter:

1. There are a number of costs, including repairs, registration and insurance, that are significant.
2. The amount that a car falls in value each year, its depreciation, is significant – particularly with new or newer cars.

Digging a little deeper

The reason for choosing to own a car is usually around independence. Whether it is the independence to drive to a job or catch up with friends, having your own car to get around supports your independence.

It is worth noting that not everyone is driving. Roy Morgan Research (2020) showed that from 2009 to 2019, fewer young Australians were driving (roymorgan.com/findings/new-data-shows-decreasing-proportion-of-younger-drivers-on-our-roads-but-more-seniors-staying-behind-the-wheel). In the 16–17 age group, only 32% of Australians were driving in 2019 (down from 35% in 2009), and in the 18–24 age group, 63% of Australians were driving, down from 70% in 2009.

As you start to think about the purchase of a car, the Royal Automobile Club of Australia (for example, the RACQ in Queensland and the RACV in Victoria) has put together a great summary document of car costs, titled Car Running Costs.

Let's use the Car Running Costs for 2022, which you can find online using a search engine. The Car Running Costs sets out the costs for a range of car models, with average running costs per year. Let's start with one of Australia's best-selling cars, the Toyota Corolla.

Ongoing costs

We mentioned towards the start of this chapter that there are two focuses: the first is understanding the ongoing costs of a car.

The Car Running Costs guide lists the ongoing costs of owning a new Toyota Corolla as being $11,410 a year – the cheapest car to own in the 'small car' category. Now, $11,410 might not sound like a lot of money, however, it is $220 per week. Therefore, if you want to own a small car like a Toyota Corolla, you need to be able to find around $200 per week, every week, to pay for it.

There is an argument that these figures are based on a new car, and that is fair enough, but there are also some costs – particularly insurance – that will be higher for young drivers.

The Car Running Costs guide also assumes that money is borrowed to buy the car – if you can save and pay cash for your car, you will save the interest those people who borrow money are paying to the bank.

Let's look at the key costs listed by the Car Running Costs guide. The biggest is the category of registration and insurance, which is listed as coming to $200 a month ($2,400 per year). It is worth doing some research on the registration cost of the car you want to buy in your state, as well as insurance costs. Insurance can be very expensive for young drivers, so know what you are getting before you start. There can be a temptation to get cheaper 'Third Party Property Damage', which only protects you for the damage caused to another car. However, if you have paid significant money for your own car, comprehensive insurance that covers your car in the event of an accident is valuable.

The next highest cost on the list is fuel: $40 a week of fuel becomes $180 over a month.

Servicing and tyres are listed at $30 per month for a new car, however, with a second-hand car it might be wiser to budget $60 per month, given that a little more maintenance is likely to be needed.

All these costs come to $440 per month – or about $100 a week (not including any car loan).

Some of these costs come as a large cost all at once. Insurance, for example, can easily be more than $1,000 for a young driver. Often, the registration renewal (maybe another $700) and insurance renewal come at around the same time, meaning you have to find some serious money quickly. Setting up an online account just for car costs, where money is regularly transferred, can help you be ready for these costs when they come.

Depreciation

The financial element of buying a car that makes it unique is 'depreciation' – this is the second focus of this chapter. Depreciation refers to the extent that something falls in value over time, and a car is likely to be the highest priced item you own that falls in value.

Going back to our Toyota Corolla example from the Car Running Costs guide, it had a price of $29,235 when new and, according to the guide, was worth $12,800 after five years. That meant it had fallen in value by $16,435 over five years, or $3,287 each year, or $63 each week.

However, we might be able to use this depreciation to our advantage. Let's assume that rather than buy the new car that falls in value by $63 each week, you buy a five-year-old second-hand Toyota Corolla for $12,800. If you keep it for five years, you might expect to be able to sell it for around $5,500. Over the five years, it will have fallen in value by $7,500, or $1,500 per year, or $29 per week.

Over five years, that is a difference of nearly $9,000, or $1,800 per year, between buying a new or five-year-old car. The five-year-old car will leave you with serious money to spend on other items.

A final word

There is no way around it – buying a car is an important financial decision because it is a significant ongoing cost and, having bought the car, it is going to fall in value.

If you understand the ongoing costs, have a plan to save regularly to meet those costs, and think about the effects of the way cars fall in value, you will be in great shape to make a sensible decision.

CHAPTER 12

Thinking about renting and moving out of home

"Home is the comfiest place to be"

– Winnie the Pooh

A note about moving out of home

This is another chapter about the 'future you'. We often hear about the challenges of renting or buying property – with both rents and property prices higher than they have been before. This chapter looks at what this might mean for you down the track.

Thinking about moving out and renting

The Australian Institute of Family Studies, in a 2019 media release titled 'More Young Adults Living at Home with their Parents', used the statistic that 43% of 20- to 24-year-olds were still living in the family home. Of course, this statistic implies that the majority of people this age (57%) had moved out of home (See https://aifs.gov.au/media/more-young-adults-living-home-their-parents).

A common first step in moving out of home is to live in a rented property with flatmates. And moving out of home is a situation that is relatively easy to start researching – an online real estate website will give you an idea of rental options. There is then another layer of costs to think about, including insurance, groceries, electricity, internet and other bills that you might choose like pay TV. The total cost of running a home might be higher than you realise. The following table is from the moneysmart.gov.au website, under an article titled 'Moving out of home'.

Ongoing costs	One-off costs
• rent • utility bills including gas, water and electricity • internet and phone bills • groceries • transport • contents insurance	• rental bond • up to four weeks rent in advance • connection fees for utilities and internet • removalist fees or van hire • furniture and homewares • parking permits

 IMPORTANT

Make sure everyone's name is on all the bills. If a bill is addressed only to you, you're the one legally responsible for paying it.

As well as recognising and budgeting for a range of costs, it is important to recognise that setting up a house involves entering into a network of contracts – for example, with the landlord, with the energy company and with the internet provider. It is very important to think carefully about the best way to set up written agreements to make sure that you and your flatmates understand the payment arrangements.

One of the worst mistakes I have seen is a person setting up a shared house and putting the bills in their own name without having any written agreement. When the flatmates left, the person was left with all the bills in their name. When they were unable to pay the bills themselves, it caused stress – this is the situation you want to guard against.

Looking ahead to buying a property

A key financial goal for a lot of people is to own a property. It was not that long ago that a property in a capital city in Australia might have cost four to five times the average wage. As I write this, the average wage (as measured by AWOTE – adult average weekly ordinary time earnings) is just over $90,000 per year with, according to investment research and data company SMQ Research, the average capital city property price being just over $1 million, making it around 11 times the average wage.

Let's assume that Alice is a young adult who wants to buy a property as a key financial goal; how can Alice work towards this in an environment where properties are expensive? Perhaps an important first point for Alice is to be realistic about where she wants to start on the property ladder. Assuming that she can start by buying a property in a suburb close to where she grew up is likely to be unrealistic. Thinking about ways that Alice can work with more realistic initial expectations, for example, being prepared to buy in a suburb further from town, to buy a house that might need some repair work or she might even buy a property with an eye to initially renting out spare rooms to generate some extra income – all of these might help make the challenge of buying a first property more manageable.

The financial building blocks that we have talked about in this book, including saving, investing and budgeting, are all building blocks that can progress Alice towards owning her own property. One of the first challenges for Alice, if she wants to be in a position to purchase a property, is saving for a deposit – the sum of money that you put towards the property you are buying alongside the loan you are likely to have to take out. Budgeting, saving and investing are all steps towards accumulating the money that can make up Alice's first home deposit.

There is a special saving scheme, called the First Home Super Saver Scheme, which might help Alice as she saves for a deposit. It allows you to put extra money of your own into the low-tax superannuation environment, and then withdraw it to use towards a deposit for a first home. The ATO website has more details on the rules of the scheme. The benefits of this scheme are that you can claim a tax deduction for the extra money you put into superannuation, and then the money in superannuation is taxed at a maximum rate of 15%. The downsides of this are the significant number of rules to understand and that the money is only to be used for a first home. As you get closer to the goal of buying a first property, it is worth considering whether this scheme has value.

One strategy that I come across more commonly involves people living at home longer and paying board to their parents while buying an investment property that they hope to move into later. There are tax advantages that come from buying a property as an investment, and the income from tenants can help pay down the mortgage.

If you are reading this as a high school student, all these are likely to be 'future you' considerations. However, if you have the future goal of owning a property in mind, good financial habits, determination and some strategic thinking, these will all be useful in getting you there, even in these times when buying a property is more challenging than it has been historically.

CHAPTER 13

Philanthropy

"No one is useless in this world who lightens the burden of others"

– Charles Dickens

A note about philanthropy

I suspect that 'philanthropy' is not a word that all high school students will have come across and, for those who are familiar with the word, will not think that it is relevant to their situation.

The definition of philanthropy is that it is helping others, usually through donations. In reality, it is usually linked to people who have significant wealth and make very large donations. For example, the article 'Australia's 50 biggest givers top $1b in donations for the first time' in *Australian Financial Review* tells of philanthropic donations like the $165 million given away in a year by the founders of accounting software company MYOB.

Annual donations such as these are beyond most young adults, however, there are three principles behind philanthropy that I want to suggest are relevant for young adults, as they think about how they might interact with others, and they are:

- Philanthropy and happiness
- Being businesslike with your generosity
- Your time matters

Philanthropy and happiness

Thinking of, and supporting the welfare of, others – whether through making donations or volunteering – seems like it is something that is very much about giving. There is, however, an interesting strand of research that suggests giving is something that leads to happiness for the person doing the giving.

Patrick Svedin (2017) wrote an article titled 'Does Giving Make you Happier, or do Happier People Give?' (usu.edu/science/discovery/fall-2017/does-giving-make-you-happy). The article starts by referring to a famous study by Elizabeth Dunn, Lara Akin and Michael Norton, where people were given smallish sums of money ($5 or $20) and split into groups where they spend that money on themselves or someone else. When the happiness of the members of the two groups was measured at the end of the experiment, those who had spent money on others were happier. Svedin looked at some other research, including scans of how people's brains work when they are donating to charity, and found that:

> *"In a nutshell, giving to charity makes us happier; especially when we freely choose to give. Whether we have a little or a lot of money, how we choose to spend it matters most to our happiness. The same is true with our time. Volunteering at a charity will do wonders for your emotional well-being. If your aim in life is for you and others to be happy, evidence suggests learning and teaching others to be deliberate in giving of their time and means to charity will have the greatest impact in this noble pursuit."*

Perhaps the perspectives that come from giving time or money to charity are behind this increased happiness – the perspective of acknowledging that we have enough that we can help others, the perspective of being able to make a positive difference when often we only hear negative stories, and the perspective of engaging with others in different situations.

Being businesslike

There are many charities that would like to have your support, whether as a volunteer or as a donor. Because of this you are in a position to be thoughtful – businesslike – in which charity or charities you want to support. You can research the services the charities provide, the amount of money they spend on overheads like offices and staff and the way they keep records of the work they do. This way you can be careful about choosing to support a charity or charities that align with your interests.

An important element to being businesslike is keeping records of any donations that you choose to make. Once you start to earn an income, a tax-deductible donation can be used to decrease your taxable income, and therefore the amount of tax that you pay. If you get into the habit of keeping your records from donations, you can pay a little less tax and have a little more money for yourself, or others, come tax time.

I have had a number of people involved in running and managing charities mention to me the preference for regular donations, for example, monthly donations. One-off donations often require time and money (for example, the cost of a mail-out or advertising), whereas regular monthly donations are more reliable and less expensive. If you find a charity that you want to support with donations, considering a small, ongoing donation might be a businesslike way to best support that charity.

Your time matters

The definition of philanthropy that we started with talked about helping others. This doesn't limit people to giving money, it can include helping others through volunteering.

As a young adult, volunteering has some key benefits beyond the already discussed tendency to make you feel happier. Hands-on volunteering provides a great opportunity to build skills and to communicate to others (for example, future employers or for university applications) the type of person that you are.

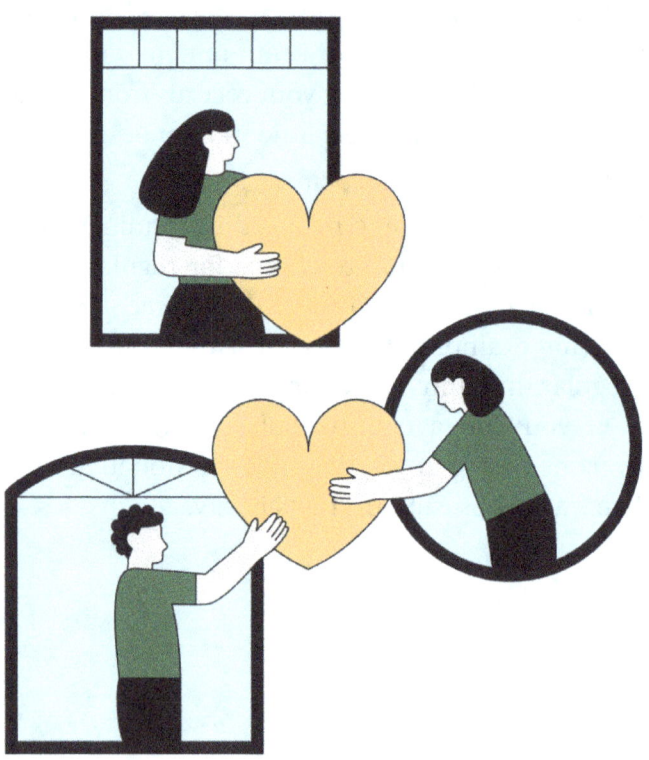

A final word

I have deliberately linked the idea of philanthropy to a group where it is not often linked – young adults. However, no one has as much time or potential to make a positive difference over a lifetime as someone who is young. As a teacher, I admire the community awareness, empathy and social justice that I see in young adults, and I encourage you to think about the potential positive difference you can make through volunteering or donating as part of your overall 'money' self.

CHAPTER 14

Gambling

"Gambling. The sure way of getting nothing for something"

– **Wilson Mizner (American playwright)**

A note about gambling

Back in the 'good old days' when I was growing up, I could not have placed a bet on a sporting competition had I wanted to. There was no gambling advertising on sport, and I don't remember TV commentators referring to the odds of sporting events in their commentary.

The Victorian Responsible Gambling Foundation put together a 2017 report titled 'Has Gambling Gatecrashed our Teens?'. In the report it highlights some statistics that are worth being aware of:

- 50% of adolescents have a high level of exposure to sports betting marketing.
- In the last 12 months, a quarter of all young people bet on sports.
- One young person in every 25 has a problem with gambling – which is one young person in every average high school classroom.
- 20% of adults with gambling problems started before they were 18 years of age.

This is the basic message of this chapter – if you want to be successful financially, avoiding gambling is the absolute best bet.

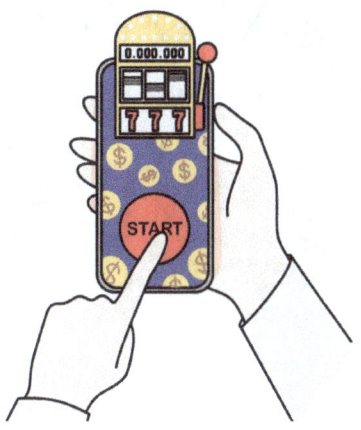

Gambling is a losing bet

The biggest gambling companies in the world, including the Australian pokies machine manufacturer, are worth billions of dollars. This is because of one simple reason: gambling is a lucrative business.

The online betting market, the games at the casino, the pokies, scratchies, lotto tickets, are all based on carefully calculated probabilities that ensures the gambler, on average, will lose.

In some ways, gambling companies are running the ultimate business. Consider pokie machines in Queensland. The Queensland Government has put together a webpage titled, 'The real odds of winning when gambling'. The webpage starts with the unambiguous statement, **'gambling odds always favour the house'** (the house being whoever is offering the bet).

As an example of the way 'gambling odds always favour the house', consider pokie machines. The same webpage says that in Queensland, pokie machines pay out 'between 85% and 92% of turnover'. That means for every $1 you put into a pokie machine, you can only expect to receive back between 85% and 92%, or in the case of $1 you receive back between 85 and 92 cents. This is a terrible value proposition – bet a dollar and, on average, lose 8 to 15 cents straight away. And this is not some vague calculation of probability – this is the carefully programmed calculation that these machines run on, just as the probability behind lotto numbers, scratchies, casino games and all gambling is carefully calculated – carefully calculated so that the house wins, and the gambler, on average, loses.

A final word

The aim of this chapter is twofold: to let you know that teenage gambling is increasingly common, and to provide you with the mathematical reality that gambling is a losing bet. When you gamble, you are on the wrong side of big companies that have carefully tilted the maths in their favour. If you find yourself struggling with gambling, get help from the adults at home, youth support services that you can find online including Kids Helpline and Gamblers Youth Helpline, your doctor or school support services.

CHAPTER 15
Experiences vs stuff

"Happiness depends upon ourselves"

– Aristotle

A note about the value of experiences

The aim of this chapter is to share some interesting research around the value of experiences.

Let's start by understanding what we mean by the terms in the title to this chapter, 'stuff' and 'experiences'.

Buying 'stuff' is about buying material possessions, for example, clothes, jewellery and furniture. Buying 'experiences' is about buying events like attending a sports game, dining out with friends or going to a concert.

There is a body of research that suggests buying experiences leads to greater happiness than buying 'stuff'. The lesson might be to be cautious about buying the latest fashion, furniture or electronics, and think more about buying experiences like travel, concerts and sporting events.

Digging a little deeper

The University of Texas (Austin), in a 2020 article, discussed the research paper, 'Spending on Doing Promotes More Moment-to-Moment Happiness than Spending on Having', published in the May 2020 issue of the *Journal of Experimental Social Psychology* by lead author Amit Kumar.

While the title of the paper suggests the core research finding, that doing (experiences) creates more happiness than having (stuff), it is worth delving a little more deeply into the method behind that finding.

The first approach saw 2,635 adults assigned to either material (stuff) or experiential group. The material group bought things such as jewellery, clothing or furniture, while the experiential shoppers attended sporting events, restaurants or other experiences (for example, movies, art galleries, theatre, concerts). Happiness was higher for participants in the experiences group, regardless of the cost of the item. A second study was done with 5,000 adults, where they were asked whether they had consumed either a material purchase (stuff) or experiential purchase (experiences) in the hour before they had been contacted. If they answered 'yes', they were then asked a series of questions about their purchase and, once again, purchasing an experience was associated with higher levels of happiness.

I suspect there might be a little bit of intuition that supports this. Most often, when asked about highlights, I notice people talking about concerts, travel, exciting sporting events and meals out. Very rarely do they talk about their new couch or big-screen TV.

Can 'stuff' be an experience?

I do wonder whether we have to be careful about being too focused on the difference between an experience and 'stuff'. For example, golf clubs would seemingly fit into the 'stuff' definition. However, for someone who really enjoys golf, then a regular game of golf is an experience.

In some ways, cars are the ultimate 'stuff' example. However, someone who really enjoys their car might have some great experiences keeping their car spotless and going for weekend drives.

Perhaps using the 'stuff' vs experiences framework could be seen as a useful guide, rather than something that has to be followed rigorously.

A final word

If you are tossing up between a new jumper and a concert ticket or thinking about whether you save up for a new TV or a holiday overseas, perhaps remembering that experiences tend to provide more happiness will be a useful framework in making decisions.

After all, I suspect the memories of great concerts, exhibitions, travel or sporting events will stay with you longer than the memory of an expensive couch or fancy rug ever will.

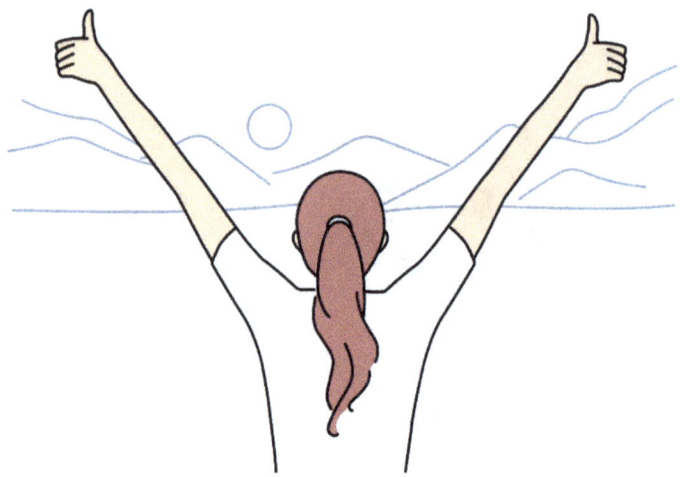

CHAPTER 16

Higher education loans program

"Education is the passport to the future, for tomorrow belongs to those who prepare for it today"

– Malcolm X

A note about a HELP loan

A key financial decision that you will make is around education, training and work experience – what knowledge and skills will you build and be able to offer employees and clients in the future?

'HELP' stands for 'higher education loans program'. A HELP loan is what many people will use to pay their 'student contribution amounts', which is their contribution to their course fees if, for example, they are studying at university.

The aim of this short chapter is to provide some understanding that a HELP loan is not as 'harsh' as a normal commercial loan (like a personal loan), and may well lead to important direct benefits including higher income earning because of your qualification, and a job that you enjoy more. If you want to study, a HELP loan might be an important solution.

Digging a little deeper

There are three important ways that a HELP Loan is less demanding than a commercial loan:

1. A HELP loan only increases by the rate of inflation.

2. It only has to be paid back with income above a certain figure.

3. The loan ends if you pass away.

Over the past 20 years in Australia (to the start of 2022), the inflation rate has been 2.38% per annum (www.macrotrends.net/countries/AUS/australia/inflation-rate-cpi). HELP loans increase each year by the rate of inflation – usually significantly less than the interest rate on a personal loan, or other commercial loan.

In the 2023/24 financial year, you only have to pay back your HELP loan if your income is above $51,550. As your income increases, you have to pay back an increasing amount to your HELP loan, starting at 1% if you earn between $51,550 and $59,518, increasing to 10% if you earn above $151,000.

Finally, if you pass away, your HELP loan does not have to be repaid by anyone else.

Add these three elements together and you have a loan that is attractive compared to commercial loans, and the student loans we hear about from other countries, like the United States.

A final word

If you are looking to study, and think that study will lead to increased job satisfaction and/or income in the future, a HELP loan might be a great way of supporting your study. Do some further research (be aware there is some misinformation out there), and see how it might work for you.

www.ingramcontent.com/pod-product-compliance
Lightning Source LLC
Chambersburg PA
CBHW050301120526
44590CB00016B/2439